WHY?

AND OTHER QUESTIONS

Robin Houghton

LIVE CANON

First Published in 2019
By Live Canon Ltd
www.livecanon.co.uk

All rights reserved

© Robin Houghton 2019

978-1-909703-77-3

WHY?

AND OTHER QUESTIONS

Robin Houghton is the author of three poetry pamphlets, *The Great Vowel Shift* (Telltale Press 2014), *Foot Wear* (2017) and *All the Relevant Gods* which won the Cinnamon Press Poetry Pamphlet competition in 2017. Her poetry appears in many magazines including *Agenda, Envoi, Magma, Poetry News, The Moth* and *The Rialto,* and anthologies including *The Best New British and Irish Poets 2017* (Eyewear). She was awarded the Poetry Society's Hamish Canham Prize in 2013. Her long-running poetry blog is robinhoughtonpoetry.co.uk. Robin worked in marketing for twenty-five years, has an MA in Digital Media and has written three books on blogging.

Acknowledgements

Thank you to the editors of the following publications in which these poems (or versions of them) previously appeared: 'Taken', *Canterbury Festival Poet of the Year Anthology 2015*; 'Long Haul', *The Interpreter's House*; 'And there was that time', *The Frogmore Papers*; 'Hat for Earrings', *The Cannon's Mouth*; 'Faux', *Coast to Coast to Coast*; 'Under Hammersmith Bridge, 2016', *The North*; 'Seeing the small picture', *Obsessed with Pipework*; 'Ladies Hour', Mary Evans Picture Library website; 'I ask what colour is the sea', *Truths, A Telltale Press Anthology*.

Contents

Cut | Burn | Poison

among extraordinary beauty grows the weed
its dirt patch the wrong colour   too stealthy
among blades all good and clean   it grows
shows teeth   develops a taste for beauty

man sharpens his tools   he cuts and digs
beauty will have a deep hole   scraped clean
dirt patch must go   dry up   stitch to scar
but what if roots are hungry   for beauty

man lights fire   burn the dark dirt patch
cauterise the blades all good and clean   sterilise
the deep deep wrong colour hole of beauty
to be saved by man   man who mixes poison

because *there must be some sacrifice*   blades
nod   weed shows teeth   while beauty   drinks

Was it the Diet Coke

offhandedly lefthandedly
drunk by the can-full
my dose of phenylalanine
my be-my-baby ringpull

was it the years of alcohol
begun in smoky boozers
limey, salty tequila shots
on tables, handled by losers

was it the bacon sarnies
the saturated fat stocking
up ooze or padding me out-
side in for a future coffin

was it the stress of work
of family of moving house
of loss of grief was it genes
or too much breathing out

was it my fault or God's
did I do wrong break a law
was it bad timing was it
me   fuck   was it me   or

Long Haul

In a bulkhead seat, in this no-place,
at no hour—Ronan stay-at-home,
Ronan friend-in-need, it's time.

Look up, Ronan

at the knock-knock of fibreglass,
like the slow chipping out of teeth.
A small grimace of rivets holds you.

Ronan face-the-wall

wallet ready, start your slide show—
Eilish on the Falls Road, smiling,
cocked foot, Brigid awake in her cot
and you nowhere, then as now—

gently through your hands go
their laughs, a rosary of images.
Pray for the pulse in your thumb
to steady the winds, go hush-a-by

Ronan daddy-come-home

Eilish with her cocked foot, Brigid
in her bed. Jesus, Mary Mother of God
and all the Saints are listening to you

Ronan fear-of-flying

Ronan nowhere over an ocean

The Retelling

After supper when all was cleared, and from
his wallet came those dog-eared photos, spread
out on the table like a royal flush,
red-eyed as always, this was his story:
first, a tremor, almost nil on a scale
of one to ten — hardly enough to tip
dull heads on pillowed necks from right to left,
certainly not to levitate a man —
then some throat opened and the long night's breath
tumbled through the lift shaft of his lungs, threw
up knives, a scything freak show in his brain.
The flapping mask, the call to brace, the prayers.
Past midnight, on a whisky, he would land;
we knew better than to reach for his hand.

Hat for Earrings

She wanted cost price—nothing more than a thin twirl of metal
that afternoon as she tweezered me out of stillness,
dripped another microgram of gold into a leather apron.
Two drops alive in her eyeglass, singing of small earlobes—
more ying-yang than half-moon, they question-marked my neck.
Each was a Rodin kiss of a piece. And I, ashamed to show
my piercings, stood at the mirror to swivel *no* but smiled
and watched myself look forward. What could I offer in return?

A soft cloche for the crown of her head, hand-dyed after hours,
slip-stitched grosgrain, a curl of feather here or there—
she chose the ribbon, the shade of felt, breathed tulle
as I cradled rhinestones. *Too much,* she said

but winked me on. This was my private work, my mistress-piece.
I saw my chance, and bartered.

Stone Man

In dunes, springing or sinking,
a sea-turtle scratched on his back,
he's one of the old guard

half in, half out.
What harried worker was dragged
from his bed to chisel this?

Plumb rule, tools at hand
thought *stone* thought *rock*
ready to stab and chip

for all his grandfathers
and for all their grandfathers
on that drab morning.

And here they are, still—
the home guard, but younger
than you think. My dad

a chip off some old block
but not yet prehistoric
him and his cronies face inland

as ribs of sand score *ocean*
behind their backs. My father
who I never saw in his apron and dagger—

massive basalt head
mouth set to secrecy and ritual
grizzled with guano, squid-ink—

rock-proud in his stillness.
It must have taken bird-men, gods,
a hundred leather-handed lads

to crab him from the quarry,
and leave him stumbled at the last
without his rod or gauge.

Seeing the Small Picture

You see, as any good cinematographer knows,
framing is a blessed skill.

Take your thumb and forefinger and make
two sides of a square.

Same with your other hand. Lift, look through.
Close one eye if you must.

Watch for long enough and all the world
will pass.

Observe the changing image outlined by skin,
by your extremities—

the art is to stay as still as if your very hands
were stretcher bars,

to look what comes: a smile, or a collared dove
perhaps, from left to right—

at what point does a raindrop cease to exist,
become the pavement?

When a trail of *Coco Mademoiselle* meets
your olfactory nerve

what word do you smell? Do your eyes water
and why?

Maybe a phrase you hoped you'd never hear
will have you pause

to imagine a body turned inside out, with all
its poke-points

turned to camera, showing what should stay contained
but can't. The body is yours.

Now freeze the image. Save. Do it all again
but smaller.

Drowning the Doves, 1916

'Last night I disposed of some type.' —T.J. Cobden-Sanderson, bookbinder and co-creator of the Doves typeface.

Metal drove him to it—spittle and tang on his palate,
a festering of taste—but who would understand?

Not the steel-jaw punch cutter, his work too good to last.
Not the two-faced partner forever waiting his chance.

This man would rather cripple himself on a bridge at night,
send his Doves to hell: dead, swaddled and tied.

From his bag, the first package—too heavy, too full—
a neap tide of toxic mud and jetsam breaks its fall.

The second, fifth, tenth slip smoothly from his hands,
descend, unravel on the current. By spring, handfuls of 'a's

and 'm's he starts to cast as seed, or throw—with hope,
like confetti—the pebbled water laughing up at him.

With each piece of type, a piece of himself also—the moon
as witness—bequeathed in bits to the river, rag and bone:

four parts sacrifice, six parts revenge. Strange how hard
it gets towards the end, his chest tight with the heaving

and the threat of the Thames already at work: whittling arms
of 't's, stroking the spines of 's's, rubbing out the dots of 'i's.

Under Hammersmith Bridge, 2016
for Robert Green

'If he wants to find it, he'll have to dive for it' —T.J. Cobden-Sanderson, bookbinder
and co-creator of the Doves typeface, 1916

I did it—at least, I paid the salvage men a century later.
I watched their seal-bodies drop overboard to sift through silt,
scrabble for fractions of metal each smaller than my fingernail,
smaller than pea teeth. Because the beauty of letters lasts longer
than the exit strategies of wronged parties. U is underwater,
horseshoe-like, for luck. E is no longer the enemy, just water
under the bridge. H is what happened, and Q is the questioning
eyes of pike and passing barge men. D is for utter devotion.
And diving. E for even now, eventually. A, alone and always.

Taken

'A Barbara Hepworth sculpture has been stolen by suspected scrap metal thieves from Dulwich Park in south London.' — BBC News, Dec 2011

This is the time of year when bones crack,
a blackout blind of sky comes down at four,

the park sighs dusk, nudges out skateboarders
shortchanged by winter. The time when three

quiet men will drink their tea, load up the van,
check each rope restraint for wear or weakness.

There's planning to this. Down by the lake
her twisted shape, two tons of displaced air

asking to be taken. She's dead weight,
a stinking fish, turning away her empty eye

as they dry-heave, nobody to hear the hiss
of the trees or the cutting gear, no-one

to witness their ragged breathing, fighting
for time, the coldness of her hips, her curved

hole forced piecemeal into square sacks.
Railway sidings would be easier to lift, and they

don't kick. Her eye socket powers curses.
Melt my body down and unlike me, you will not

be missed by the wideangle view, nor the sun
nor by those who come to hear birds, nor the air.

Captain Hotine calls for retriangulation

Let's throw our nets over the pointed heads of forests,
cathedral spires, follies, granite boulders upon boulders,
all the rocky peaks you breathe heavily to reach on foot
with rope, knapsack, cigs, oily socks. Take a pickaxe.
Windcheater. Steam up your boots, carry your theodolite
up through the boggy stenchlands, the howling places.
Imagine this country as it is: the finest mesh of lines
straight as Roman roads, a reduction of distances, angles.
Ours is a set of bonny concrete pillars, a numbers game
where time is not here and certainly not there, where
each jotting down by hand forms one mighty thread.
Pause on each panopticon hill, set out your gear, picture
this planet's curve from above. Breathe out, wait for night.

Note: The process of placing trig points on top of prominent hills and mountains began in 1935 to assist in the accurate retriangulation of Great Britain. Martin Hotine is credited with designing the pillars and directing the operation. Trig points have been redundant since the mid-1990s. (Ordnance Survey blog, 2016)

'His hope was a waking dream'

'Man falls into Anish Kapoor art installation of 8ft hole painted black'
—The Guardian, 21-8-18

he wanted to go quickly
he wanted to step lightly out of the light
out of the outside in

he wanted to step backwards
no-light was calling him and his eyes lied
gravity took him

into the inside out he went
into his waiting absence he stepped lightly
into blacker than him

he went into limbo
the dark was calling him and his feet lied
the hole took him

he wanted to step quickly
he absented the light and his body gave way
into nothing in it

he fell in love with nothing
he fell into lies and he wanted to go in
out of the outside in

I ask what colour is the sea

I find it greyscale of gull belly caught in a squint, a hint of gravestone.
Some days a sick greenish grey. But I ask the world and it says *blue*.

Some days I see a red horizon, its neat cut staunched by blotting paper,
a frieze of container ships like comedy castles, a spot of shadow play.

Still grey. I summon the usual references—squirrel tail, raincloud,
mushroom, beard—break them into cyan, magenta, yellow, key—

place them on a colour wheel, print ten copies and then another ten.
I look again. Is it a pea-green soup I ask, or is it pearl-diver black?

Is it a pinot grigio of pulped tabloids, or the matt of coal scuttle?
In the songs it's always blue. In the songs the sun shines and the sky

is also blue, but today, grey. Gone are the ships and the heavy payload,
gone is the type metal and the gun metal. The pearl divers are gone.

It's greyer than the faces of night visitors and all their apologies.
It's greyer than what a cat sees in the dark on a moonless night.

When I ask *what colour is the sea* I don't ask what colour the crowbar
or coffin lid or oracle. They are whatever I see, or say—even grey.

Missed

There are five of us in this taxi and my phone rings.
The couple in front chat with the driver and my husband holds my hand.
My brother is calling me from another country and he's with my mother.
The driver sees my face in the rearview mirror and he knows.
The plane won't wait for me and we are hours from the airport.
The driver is speeding and the couple in front are chatting.
My brother's voice is strange and I don't know what to say to him.
My husband holds my hand and we are hours from the airport.
The couple in front are whispering and the driver is speeding.
My mother had asked when I'd be back but she didn't wait for me.
I will write about this one day. Maybe I'll change the ending.

And there was that time

she took us all to the shops
and left my brother sleeping in his pram
outside the greengrocers
she was halfway home before remembering—
at least, that's how my sister tells it
in that semi-comedic way
wanting perhaps to draw a line
from there to here, prefiguring a mind
that would gradually free itself of burdens,
go back to the blank map of babyhood.

I prefer to think of her in black and white
kicked back on a deckchair on Hastings Pier
neat white revers on the neckline
of her gingham dress
pregnant and laughing
as my father took the photo.

Faux

here is the shop
where you bought me a fur

three blocks west
of Andrássy út   in this alley
papered with agitprop

I wear your mother tongue
poorly   I am graceless
as a child in stilettos

nothing left of the beast
but its packaging   and the heart
still in it

hung on my neck   its bloodied head
trailed guts   like loose threads
across the city   led me home

when ice floes formed
under the Chain Bridge
it purred   *keep warm*

some days it begged to be petted
by strangers   to be freed
un-mink me

you bought me a fake
here is the shop

Old business

why do I keep looking at
keep looking

this email
why did he hit send

every word starts with
his name

a lower case letter   even
that means something

he's learned something
something

he wants
some kind of tragedy

has crushed him
he's a broken man

some woman broke him
he must remember

that time when
in our different accents

we said the word *friends*
both fake

we exchanged ourselves
unwanted

in an instant, like
Christmas presents

we left the meeting
left the conversation

we left   the hotel
behind the headboard

in three-nineteen
all in lower case

I nearly left a note
but did I

I have googled him

I wish I hadn't

Ladies' Hour

It's good for the bust
just a gentle stretch or two
then small steps in

it's warmer than you think
it's deeper than you think
I love the blue fear of this—

down, down — watching my leg
disappear, and the other,
in up to my waist, my neck—
that's it—

between me and the sea
just the smell of steerage,
the low belly of boat, the swell.

It's good for the bust.
I will do this. Reach forward,
take a breath. I believe

I will float, I will glide,
just a push with my foot,
my little foot, and let go

Note: A 1912 White Star Line brochure for the RMS Titanic depicts a swimming bath on one of the middle decks. (Reference 10213847 at the Mary Evans Picture Library)